The Go for No!® Leader Workbook

Richard Fenton
& Andrea Waltz

This Workbook Belongs to:

Published by

www.SuccessIn100Pages.com

ISBN 978-1-947814-70-7

Copyright © Richard Fenton & Andrea Waltz, 2020

All rights reserved.

When average people hear the
word 'NO' they think the
process is over.

When top performers hear 'NO'
they think things are just
getting started.

-Richard Fenton & Andrea Waltz

It has been said that the word 'NO' has destroyed more lives than all the wars since the dawn of time. We believe this to be true. But it doesn't have to be that way. Not for you—and not for your team.

Introduction

Everyone loves the sound of the word, YES! It's so positive, so empowering. And then there's NO. For most people, NO is just the opposite—negative, draining, the antithesis of YES. But what if everyone's wrong? What if <u>NO</u> could actually be the most empowering word in the world? What if you could achieve every quota, hit every income goal—and, perhaps, reach every personal dream—by simply learning to hear NO more often?

As kids we weren't fazed at all when we heard NO—we shrugged it off, laughed at it, flicked it away like a bug. But somewhere along the line our natural sense of tenacity gets lost. Or, worse, it is drummed

out of us by well-meaning parents, teachers, and society in general.

But, what if, *starting today,* you could help your people get that tenacity back? What if the word NO stopped stopping them? What if the word NO actually started empowering your team rather than demoralizing them? What if every time your people hear the word 'NO' they become stronger, more powerful and more resilient? And what if the unthinkable happened, and hearing NO' actually started being (dare we say)... fun?

That's what the Go for No! program is designed to do: to make people think about 'NO' in a radically different way, challenging your assumptions and beliefs in the process. And while you may not agree with everything we share in the Go for No! program, we can assure you these concepts are proven to be effective. In fact, if we're successful, we'll help make the word 'NO' one of the most empowering words in your business.

Removing a Major "Restrainer"

A great analogy for understanding the role Go for No! plays is based around the two ways to move a vehicle forward.

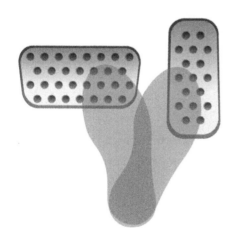

The <u>first</u> way is obvious: simply put your foot <u>on</u> the gas.

The <u>second</u> is not so obvious, which is by taking your foot <u>off</u> the brake!

The problem for most people is they focus the majority of their attention on learning new skills to accelerate performance—in other words, hitting the gas. But then they find themselves disappointed when the results they hoped for fail to appear. The reason, of course, is that while they were focused on hitting the gas, they forgot to take their other foot off the brake! The engine is revving like mad, but they're spinning their wheels and going nowhere fast.

On the other hand, if they'd simply taken their foot off the brake, they'd have moved forward. In other words, more selling skills is like hitting the gas. Learning to deal with the fear of rejection is like taking your foot off the brake.

The Five Failure Levels

The Go for No! program is designed to move people through the following Five Failure Levels:

The Five Failure Levels:

Perhaps the best place to start is with a quick review of what we call "The Five Failure Levels."

Level #1) The Ability to Fail.

Everyone on planet earth has the ability to fail. It's where we all start! What keeps most people at level-one status is their intense desire to avoid any form of failure at all costs. As a result, 80% of all people never move past this basic level.

Level #2) The Willingness to Fail.

Level-two people develop the willingness to fail, which means they come to accept failure as a natural by-product of the process of seeking success. Fewer than 20 percent of all people make it to level two for any sustained period of time.

Level #3) The Wantingness to Fail.

The biggest mental leap for most people is getting to a place where they stop tolerating NO as a necessary evil that must be dealt with in order to succeed, and they actually *want* to hear NO more often—where they develop the desire to increase the amount of failure they experience with the inner faith that personal and financial growth will follow. Fewer than 5 percent of all people ever get to this all important third level.

Level #4) Failing Bigger and Faster.

The people who ascend to level four are those who have come to the conclusion that if failing is good, then failing faster is better. And not just failing faster—if one is going to increase their failure rate, they should do it going after big goals that are worthy of the effort. Which leads us to where <u>YOU</u> come in…

Level #5) Failing Exponentially.

This final level is a function of leadership through multiplication of effort. After all, if hearing NO more often can increase individual success, then getting <u>everyone</u> to fail more will lead to group (or team) success.

A Slant Toward "Selling"

While Go for No! is not exclusively a "sales" course, per se, you will notice there is a definite slant toward "SELLING" with the terms sales and salesperson used often. There are two reasons for this:

- First, most of the people who participate in the program are, by title, *salespeople*.
- And second, even if they are not "salesperson" by title (recruiters, for example) they experience rejection on a regular basis. In short, anyone who is alive on this planet is engaged in "selling" whether they call it that or not. Everyone sells.

So, while this program is very much about selling, it is by no means only for salespeople. It's for anyone who has to face failure and rejection to get what they want in business and/or in life—which is pretty much everyone. And, for simplicity, we'll be using the term "Team Leader" rather than "Sales Manager" since this guide will be used in such a wide variety of industries and professions.

Go for No!® Survey Results

We surveyed over four hundred business professionals about their fears and motivations and the results were eye-opening.

First, we asked: **What is the biggest fear on the part of a salesperson?**

- 51% said that the customer would say no and reject them.
- 22% said upsetting people by coming across pushy or aggressive.
- 18% said not making the sale or reaching their sales goal.
- Amazingly, only 9% said they were concerned that the product was right for the customer.

Next, we asked: **What is the #1 quality of a great salesperson?**

- 38% said the willingness to face rejection.
- 22% said ability to close the sale.
- 18% said communication and negotiation skills.
- Only 5% said product knowledge!

Finally, we asked: **When it comes to dealing with rejection in sales, which is most difficult: making the first call on a prospect, or following up with someone who has already told you NO?**

- 27 percent said making the initial contact call.
- 37% said following-up with someone who had already said 'NO' to them in the past.

Let it suffice to say the fear of failure and rejection costs businesses billions of dollars every year. You could make the case that this is their problem, not yours. If they don't perform, just get someone else. There are a couple of issues with this line of thinking.

Problem #1: Unwanted Turnover Is Expensive

When you consider the cost of hiring and training new employees, increasing turnover is not the solution. Factor in open positions and the problem becomes even worse. What's interesting is, the fact that people quit jobs or are terminated for inadequate performance is not the problem—it's the <u>result</u> or <u>consequence</u> of the problem. The problem is *why* they quit or are terminated.

On the surface it's easy to say it was their inability to perform. Okay, true enough. But the bigger question is: *Why* were they unable to perform? This is the question that gets to the root of the problem.

In the vast majority of cases, the reason people fail to perform is almost always due to "call reluctance" as a result of an inability to deal with failure and rejection. Or, dare we say, to <u>not</u> deal with it.

It's easy to deal with numbers: numbers are right there, in black and white. That's why we love numbers—because they're measureable. Fear, on the other hand, is not easily measurable. Which makes it easy to ignore. But should you decide to ignore this problem, you'll be doing so at your own peril and at significant expense.

Problem #2: Fearful People <u>Will</u> Make Their Way Onto Your Team

Wouldn't it be great if everyone on your team was fearless? Well, forget it—unless you have a very small team and you're very lucky, that's not going to happen. Why? Because, statistically, there are not enough "fearless" people in the world (estimated to be less than 10 percent of the working population) from which organizations can hire. Even with the most sophisticated testing and screening process, people with the fear of failure and rejection <u>will</u> make their way onto your team. Rejection-averse performers must be recruited, too, and then reprogrammed to overcome their resistance to hearing 'NO' until they can get results and achieve success.

Skill vs. Mindset

There are two primary ways that leaders help people to be successful in sales:

- The first is making sure they have the necessary <u>skills</u> to be successful (for example, prospecting, gathering information, presenting features/benefits, overcoming objections, closing deals, getting referrals, etc.)

- The second is helping them cultivate and develop the <u>mindset</u> necessary for using these skills (in this case, we're talking about being able to deal effectively with failure and rejection.)

Most leaders spend the vast majority of their time on the former (skills), while spending very little time on the latter (mindset).

This is not to say that you, as a leader, shouldn't spend time teaching selling skills—of course you should. But quite often the focus is on skills to the exclusion of mindset. This is a serious mistake.

No matter how much training a leader provides to their people on strategies and techniques for getting to 'YES', most of their time will still be spent hearing, 'NO' and dealing with the adverse effects on their performance over time. Pretending 'NO' doesn't exist changes nothing—the problem doesn't just go away.

No matter how talented and skilled, your people <u>will</u> be told NO.

NO is inevitable.

Damage Over Time

Over time, the word 'NO' chips away at motivation and drains energy. And when heard often enough, the word 'NO' often leads to decreased prospecting activity, which leads to a decrease in sales. Which leads to a decrease in motivation. And on and on. Until performance comes to a standstill Or they quit. *Or you're forced to let them go.*

As such, it makes sense to not only address the issue head on, but also to find ways to make 'NO' work *for* you rather than against you.

"What if we don't change at all ... and something magical just happens?"

If every prospect your people approached said yes to every offer, you wouldn't need to pay them very much. Yet, in reality, salespeople are some of the highest paid individuals in the world.

So when you think about it, you aren't really paying your people to hear yes—you're paying them to hear 'NO.'

Can You Empty Your Cup?

Many people find the Go for No! concept to be somewhat counter-intuitive, forcing them to think in a different way. Which reminds us of the story about the Zen master and student in search of knowledge.

The Zen master is pouring tea as the student rambles on and on, trying to impress the Zen master with all the things he already knew. As the student is talking, he notices that the Zen master has not only filled his cup to the top, he continues pouring until the tea begins spilling onto the table. The student exclaimed, *"Zen master, can you not see the cup is overflowing?"* The Zen master replied, *"You are like the cup, full to the top with what you already know. To learn something new, one must first be willing to empty their cup."*

When people go through our training, we tell them this story and ask them to empty their cups and set aside their beliefs about failure and rejection. In the same way, we ask *you* to empty *your* cup, too.

The Beginning, Not the End

Finally, before you dig into the guide, we want you to know that we consider this the beginning of the journey together, not the end. We'd love to answer any questions you may have, and your feedback is both welcome and greatly appreciated. We're here to assist you in any way we can, so please do not hesitate to contact us.

To your success,

Richard Fenton & Andrea Waltz
Program creators, keynoters, and #1 bestselling authors of *Go for No!*®

The Six Go for No!® Leadership "Performance Drivers"

▼

Performance Driver #1

Communicate the Go for No! Concept Every Chance You Get

▼

Performance Driver #2

Change the Negative Stigma People Have Around "Selling"

▼

Performance Driver #3

Coach Your People Rather than Just "Cheering" Them On

▼

Performance Driver #4

Challenge Your People Out of Their "Comfort Zones"

▼

Performance Driver #5

Celebrate Success "Behaviors" Even When They Fail to Deliver Results

▼

Performance Driver #6

Commit to the Process & "Walk-the-Talk"

Go for No!® Leader Performance Driver #1

Communicate the Go for No!® Concept Every Chance You Get

Before we continue, we're going to assume you've completed our online course. At a minimum you've heard us speak or read our book, because having an understanding of the Go for No! concept is an <u>absolute</u> <u>requirement</u> to implementing it and reinforcing it. **Communication starts with consumption**.

Imagine you're standing around with a group of co-workers who are having a conversation about a popular TV series or movie—one you haven't seen. You want to participate in the conversation, but you can't—all you can do is stand there and listen. Worse, you decide to fake it by saying, *"Oh, I love that series!"* It works for a little while, until someone asks you a question—a question you are unable to answer.

Oops. You've been found out. Everyone knows the truth now: *you're a pretender.* This can't be allowed to happen. If it does, your credibility gets destroyed.

To teach something, you <u>must</u> know it. In this way, getting the most from your team starts with you. The more you know it—and the more you *do* it—the better a Go for No! leader you can be.

Communicate Early and Often

Communication should start immediately after your team is exposed to the Go for No!® concept. Failing to do so suggests their involvement isn't all that important. If so, the training will have been only 20% effective (more on this later.) You don't want only 20% of the team's performance to be impacted—you want everyone's performance to be improved.

Legendary Chicago Mayor, Richard J. Daley, was famous for having coined the phrase, *"Vote early, and vote often."* When it comes to communicating Go for No!®, the rule is the same: *Communicate early and communicate often.*

In terms of where to communicate, there are a number of key opportunities where Go for No!® should be mentioned and discussed, including:

- Team meetings
- Conference calls
- Newsletters
- Emails
- One-on-one conversations
- Collaborative platforms (Slack, etc.)
- Social Media

And again, it's helpful to make sure the Go for No!® topic is mentioned early—near the top of the call, at the top of the email or newsletter, etc.—to keep the subject top-of-mind, not simply as an afterthought.

Align Go for No!® with the Organization's Strategic Objectives

At the present moment, your organization probably has any number of strategic objectives (for example, executing a new product roll out, reducing excessive spending, increasing market share, etc.) No matter what these strategic objectives may be, the key underlying long-term goal is always the same—which is increasing profit.

Profit is any company's reason for existence, and sales will always be a central element in achieving that goal.

As such, Go for No! must always be communicated in a way that demonstrates an alignment with people's day-to-day jobs and the organization's objectives, not in conflict with them.

Make it clear that Go for No! is not designed to make people fail more for failure's sake—it's to help them reframe the way they think about failure and rejection so they can be <u>more</u> successful, not less successful. The purpose of the program is NOT to only get more NOs—it's to hear YES more often, too. It's to <u>increase</u> sales, not decrease them. Put another way:

'YES' <u>is</u> the destination, but
'NO' is how you get there.

There should be no confusion around this.

Encourage Two-Way Communication

Another objective should be the encouragement and facilitation of communication in both directions. Encourage your people to share their opinions about the concept, and to express any issues they may be having. In other words, don't talk *at* people, talk with them.

One of the ways to encourage two-way communication is through the power of storytelling.

Stories make any concept more understandable, relatable, and interesting. Facts and figures are easily forgotten, while stories are easier to remember—especially stories that show results, or at least progress. As such, people should get the opportunity to share their Go for No! stories—the good, the bad, and even the ugly.

Invite people to share their experiences going for no on calls, at meetings, or by writing an article for the team/company newsletter.

Otherwise reluctant players are more likely to get onboard with the program if they can relate to it through the experiences of fellow team members. And this includes you. What experiences have you had while going for no? Share your stories, too. This helps make what might still be an abstract concept real for people who, up to that point, just don't get it.

Lastly, Be Empathetic

As you go, don't be surprised when some people struggle with the process. While Go for No! is designed to help everyone on the team achieve higher levels of performance, it is particularly important for the most failure/rejection averse among your team.

When this happens, remember to be empathetic. Take off your "leader hat" and put on your "friend hat" for a moment in order to understand what they're struggling with. Show you care.

This doesn't mean they are not accountable for their results and achieving quotas (if quotas are part of their responsibility.) They are. None of that changes. But if you want people to open-up to you and share their issues and feelings, they need support, not scorn. Telling people "it's easy" and to "just do it" does not help. Work to see the issue through their eyes.

Analysis & Action Steps
for Performance Driver #1...

- On a scale of 1-10, how would you rate your current understanding of the *Go for No!* concept?

  1   2   3   4   5   6   7   8   9   10

  Poor   Excellent

*If you rated yourself anything below a "7" it is critical that you read the book if you've yet to do so, at a minimum, and ideally complete the *Mastering Go for No!®* online course.

- List at least six (6) ways you intend to communicate the *Go for No!* concept to your team:

1) _____

2) _____

3) _____

4) _____

5) _____

6) _____

Go for No!® Leader Performance Driver #2

Change the Negative Stigma Around "Selling"

▼

Few people dreamed about being a salesperson when they were ten years old: astronaut, cowboy, fireman, yes—movie star, ballerina, baseball player, absolutely—but sales? No way. This isn't because there's anything wrong with being in sales (when done right), it's just not as glamourous or exciting. And we didn't ask for sales training for Christmas, and you've probably never had a kid show up at your door at Halloween dressed as a used car salesman.

The interesting thing is that the largest profession in the world just happens to be selling. What's more, it's one of the highest paid. But, sadly, it also ranks consistently among the ten most hated. The ironic part is that the world needs salespeople more than virtually any other profession.

So why has a profession so important and highly paid as sales developed such a bad reputation? It's simple. It's because of negative experiences with pushy salespeople who lied, tricked and/or pressured you and sold you something you didn't want. That's it. There's no other reason. Even most salespeople hate salespeople.

That said, why would you want your team to *go for no,* knowing that feeling manipulated and pressured is part of what people hate about salespeople?

The truth is, people don't hate salespeople—they hate self-centered, highly-manipulative, fast-talking, stereotypical "snake oil" salespeople who care only about making the sale and not about them. And they only hate being manipulated and pressured when the product or service doesn't benefit them.

Conversely, people love and appreciate good salespeople who help them buy products and services that change their lives for the better. They appreciate them so much that they go back and buy from them over and over again.

The key to overcoming the negative internal stigma people carry about "being in sales" is to help them reframe the way they perceive what they do—from a self-centered "salesperson" to a customer-centered "sales consultant" who operates with the prospect's interest in mind while ensuring the goal of making the sale is also achieved.

What Does "Selling" Mean to Your People?

Here's a great way to get inside the heads of the people on your team. Ask them to finish this sentence:

"SELLING" is...

_____(fill in the blank)_____.

You're going to get answers that fall into one of three categories:

1. Answers that are "<u>results</u>" oriented
2. Answers that are "<u>relationship</u>" oriented
3. Answers that contain equal amounts of <u>both</u>.

The only approach that will guarantee long-term sales success is #3 in which the person understands the goal of every interaction is to make

---

the sale while simultaneously ensuring customer satisfaction. It's never one or the other. It's always both.

The Four Selling Styles

There are two primary concerns that drive most sales behavior. They are:

- **RESULTS** (making the sale and generating profit/income)

- **RELATIONSHIPS** (customer satisfaction with the process)

When you cross-reference these two concerns, from Low to High, there are four very distinct "selling styles" that emerge:

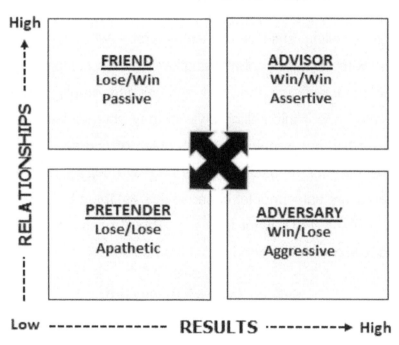

Let's look at each, one at a time:

Selling Style #1 (lower right)

THE <u>ADVERSARY</u>

While we wish it weren't true, there are actually salespeople who go into every interaction with the attitude that what is taking place is a battle—a *war of wills* in which either they or the prospect will emerge victorious. Their goal is to "WIN" the sale, even if it means that the customer has to LOSE in the process. This may require them to be aggressive and manipulative, which is fine as long as they achieve their goal, which is to make the sale at all costs. These are the people most responsible for creating the negative selling stigma that haunts customers, prospects and other salespeople alike.

Selling Style #2 (upper left)

THE <u>FRIEND</u>

The second selling style is the salesperson who goes into every interaction with ultimate goal of being seen as the customer's friend—even if it means losing the sale and leaving empty handed. The saddest thing about this selling style is they actually believe that <u>not</u> selling the customer is helping them, which of course, it isn't. These are the people most impacted by the negative selling stigma created by high-pressure salespeople, because the last thing they want is for a prospect to think that's what *they* are. They'll pass on the sales if it means they leave feeling good about themselves.

Selling Style #3 (lower left)

THE <u>PRETENDER</u>

This is the saddest selling style of all because they have no objective other than being paid. They are simply *pretending* to be salespeople. The paycheck is all that matters, for as long as they can get it. Once you catch on that they are serving no one's interest other than their own, they're let go—only to land in another sales job for another unsuspecting employer. They bring NO redeeming value to anyone. Their presence is the ultimate lose/lose.

Selling Style #4 (upper right)
THE ADVISOR

Finally, we come to the ultimate of all selling styles: the person who goes into every interaction with the attitude that both parties must walk out winners for them to have done their job properly. Win/win is the only acceptable option. They ask great questions, determine needs, and once they have, they'll advise the customer to buy—which might require them to be assertive, but never aggressive. They believe that if the product/service being offered improves the customer's condition, they *go for no.* To take it a step further, when a true need has been established, they consider not selling the customer to be a *disservice.* As such, the trusted advisor model of selling is what all salespeople should strive to emulate.

Encourage the "Advisor Style" Minimizes the Stigma

Go for No! is a process—a tool—that can be used to club a prospect over the head when in the wrong hands, but also one that can be used to create a win-win when used in the customer's best interest. To be clear: this is the ONLY way we suggest you and your people use it. Helping your people align themselves with the "Advisor" sales model helps people not only remove the negative stigma around selling, it allows them to see themselves as part of the solution rather than part of the problem. This is also a critical element part of successfully implementing Go for No! as a part of your selling culture.

Analysis & Action Steps
for Performance Driver #2...

- On a scale of 1-10, how would you define the issue of "selling stigma" for the members of your team?

  1   2   3   4   5   6   7   8   9   10

  Not a Big Issue   A Major Issue

*If you answered anything above a "6", in what ways do you plan to work with your team to help them let go of their stigma around selling?

- List up to six (6) people on your team that you believe have issues with "selling" as something they do "to" people rather than "for" them:

1) _____

2) _____

3) _____

4) _____

5) _____

6) _____

Go for No!® Leader Performance Driver #3

Coach Your People Rather than Just "Cheering" Them On

There are three primary objectives of coaching:

1... To facilitate the learning process.

2... To create behavior change.

3... To achieve goals and drive results.

Which of these three objectives is most important? This is not a trick question—the correct answer is #3. Achieving goals and driving results are the primary role of a team leader. And how do you reach goals and drive results?

The answer is through #1 and #2.

If you don't coach your people, they do not gain new skills. They repeat the same ineffective behaviors over and over without even realizing it. As such, coaching is critical to performance improvement and team success. In the end, it may well be the most important thing a team leader does.

Sadly, according to one study, 73% of managers spend less than 5% of their time coaching their sales teams. *(Source: TAS Group.)* Worse still, some team leaders don't coach their people at all.

Why Team Leaders Don't Coach

The top three reasons team leaders give for not providing coaching to their people (in order) are:

1. They don't have time.

2. They don't believe it matters.

3. They don't know how.

And even when they *do* provide coaching, the majority of coaching provided is *reactive* in nature, once a performance issue has reached a critical level. Unfortunately, fewer than 2% of salespeople will ask for help, even when they're struggling. Why? Because they fear looking weak. They feel embarrassed. They feel lost. So they'll continue on, silently stumbling and struggling, hoping no one notices—which of course you do notice.

"I suppose I'll be the one to mention the elephant in the room."

The truth is, it is not the team member's job to ask for help, it's your job to provide it. <u>You</u> need to make time.

Now, we're not going to pretend that we can turn you into a highly effective coach in a few pages in a workbook. If your organization provides training on coaching, that's great. But if not, it's up to you to seek the training you need in the form of workshops, courses—and perhaps to even hire a coach to coach you on coaching. It's that important.

Coaching At Its Best

The term "coaching" is often misunderstood, so let's start by getting clear on what we think coaching is and isn't:

- It's not setting goals and quotas—*that's communication.*

- It's not teaching features and benefits—*that's training.*

- It's not delivering performance reviews (if that's something you're responsible for)—*that's management.*

- And it's not telling people things like *"You can do it!"* and *"Let's make it happen!"—that's cheerleading.*

There's nothing wrong with any of the tasks listed above: each is important, and they all need to be done. But they're not the deep level *coaching* required to achieve goals and drive results.

Climbing Into the Other Person's Head

Great coaching never starts with an attack or with criticism. It starts by asking critical questions to gain an understanding of what's going on in the other person's mind—to climb into their head and see the world through their eyes.

"Wait a minute," you're probably thinking. *"I'm a team leader, I wasn't hired to be a therapist!"* Are you sure about that?

Selling isn't just a skill, it's also a mindset. You must figure out what's going on inside someone's mind if you want to impact results. This is especially true when it comes helping people with issues of failure and rejection.

It is with this in mind that we offer the following collection of coaching questions, each designed to help you diagnose issues and get a glimpse into someone's mindset:

Group #1: Questions About Emotional Reaction to "NO"

- *What do you <u>THINK</u> when you hear several NOs in a row? How do you <u>FEEL</u> when you hear a series of NOs? What do you <u>DO</u> when you get a lot of no's in a row?*
- *On a scale of 1-10 (with 1 being best, and 10 being the worst) what is your current level of negative emotional reaction to getting a no?*

Group #2: Questions About Perception of "Failure" and "Success"

- *When you think about the word "failure" what comes to mind?*
- *How easy or difficult is it for you to separate the concept of "failing" from "being a failure?"*

Group #3: Questions About "NO-Awareness"

- *How are you currently tracking your NOs? If you're not tracking your NOs, why not?*
- *How many NOs did you personally obtain yesterday? Last week? Last month? For the year?*
- *Tell me about a time in the past month when you pursued a NO and it eventually became a yes?*

Group #4: Questions About Understanding Opportunities to Hear "NO"

- *What are 5-6 Go for No! opportunities during the sales, service and/or recruiting process?*
- *How consistently are you following up with qualified prospects that have told you NO in the past?*
- *How many prospects do you currently have in your pipeline?*
- *What are you doing to get <u>more</u> prospects in your pipeline?*

Group #5: Questions About Going After BIG NOs

- *Who are the "biggest" prospects you've approached in the last 30-60 days?*
- *When's the last time you followed up on someone who gave you a BIG NO in the past?*
- *Who do you have on your prospect list that you've hesitated to call? Why have you waited?*

Group #6: Questions About the "Value" of NO

- *Have you taken the time to calculate the dollar value of every NO you hear?*
- *If so, what is it? If not, why not?*

Group #7: Questions About Making Assumptions

- *Tell me about a time when you made an assumption about a prospect or customer's ability or desire to buy, and your assumption turned out wrong?*
- *How often do you find yourself making decisions for others by prejudging their willingness or ability to buy <u>now</u>?*
- *Have you considered that by assuming the customer won't buy that you are, in effect, saying 'NO' for them?*

Group #8: Questions About Persistence

- *What qualified prospects have you failed to follow up with? How long has it been since you last called on them?*
- *What are your reasons for giving up on someone, even though you know they are a qualified prospect?*
- *Are you worried about "stepping over the line" with a prospect? What do you fear might happen if you accidently do?*

Not every question listed on the previous pages may be appropriate for you and your business, and you'll probably come up with other great questions to ask. But it's a good list to start with.

Drilling Down to "How"

There's an interesting story about Christopher Columbus, documented in a book by Girolamo Benzoni, in 1565.

As the story goes, Columbus was attending a dinner with a group of Spanish noblemen. Eventually, the conversation turned to Columbus' discovery of the Americas, and it didn't take long for Columbus to realize the men were not impressed when he overheard one of the noblemen say to another, "Given enough time, any one of them could have done what Columbus did."

Rather than take offense, Columbus asked a servant to go to the kitchen and bring him a hard-boiled egg, which intrigued everyone at the table. When the egg arrived Columbus wagered that none of the men could make the egg stand up on its end. The egg was passed around the table, and one by one each man attempted the task. They all failed.

When the egg got back around to Columbus, he smacked one end of the egg on the table, flattening it, then he balanced the egg on the flattened end. Columbus said, "Yes, gentlemen, it *is* possible for any of you to have discovered the New World—even easy, perhaps—because everything is easy once someone has shown you how."

This story is so well known that a monument in the shape of an enormous egg standing on its flattened end was erected in Florence, Italy, to celebrate it.

In the spirit of the Columbus story, our definition of coaching is:

> *Getting results through others, not only by telling them <u>what</u> to do and why they should do it, but also showing them <u>how</u>.*

In other words, coaching isn't simply telling people "what" to do—it's showing them "how." For example: Imagine a coach helping a baseball player who is in a hitting slump. Pointing out that the player is in a slump doesn't help—they already know they're in a slump, they want to know <u>how</u> to get out of it. Telling them to "get more hits" or "increase your batting average" doesn't help—they want to be shown <u>how</u> to do it. They want someone to take them to the cage and show them how to do things differently. It's about showing people how. Because everything is easier when someone shows you <u>how</u>.

Don't just tell your people what to do—*show them how.*

Thank you, Columbus.

Don't Coach the Team, Coach Individuals

Coaching your team is a misnomer in that you can't coach the *team* since each player has specific, individual needs. You must work with people one on one, or buddy performers up where they provide the coaching.

Assign a "NO-Buddy™"

You must drive performance *through* your team if you are going to achieve your goals. No matter how Herculean your coaching efforts may be, you cannot coach every person to the degree they may require.

A great method for helping team members improve performance without having to do the coaching yourself is to pair people with what we refer to as a "NO-Buddy" to encourage, coach, and hold each other accountable to the NO-Goals they have set. In this way you are not the person doing the coaching; you are merely the person coordinating and facilitating it.

There are two ways you can pair people up and they each have their advantages and disadvantages.

1) Pair people based on similarities of performance, time in the organization, skill level, etc. so that they are on an equal playing field.

Advantages: comfort for the participants.

Disadvantages: Perhaps limited growth as they are on the same level.

2) Pair up people who are radically different such as a seasoned experienced person with a newbie.

Advantages: each person will be challenged as the seasoned person will be forced to teach some fundamentals, and the new person or poorer performer will be challenged to keep up.

Disadvantages: both could get a little frustrated since they are not operating at the same performance level.

No matter how people pair up, NO-Buddies should:

- Communicate their NO-Goals with each and decide how often they'll compare notes on their results.

- Talk about the challenges, opportunities, and wins they've experienced.

- Encourage each other to stay positive and persistent and celebrate both successes and failures.

In the fast-paced environment of your job, sales coaching often gets squeezed out. It shouldn't. You must make time to develop people. This is especially true when it comes to overcoming psychological fears of failure and rejection.

Trust and Empathy

For your coaching efforts to work, remember you must earn trust. This starts by taking off your leader hat and putting on your coaching hat and engaging in coaching conversations in as non-judgmental a way as possible. Telling someone their fear of rejection is stupid and to just "get over it" will not lead to behavior change. Be empathetic and listen before you speak.

Let Them Create the Solution

Telling people how to improve their performance is critical to success,

 but what's even better is when the person you're working with feels they made the decision themselves. No one likes to be told what to do, so don't—ask them what changes they're going to make. Make the

behavior changes *their* idea. Make sure people walk away from the coaching conversation owning the solution.

Analysis & Action Steps
for Performance Driver #3...

- Review the eight groups of coaching questions in this section and CIRCLE 8-10 that you feel would be great questions to use with the members of your team.

- Which members of your team do you feel might benefit from having a NO-Buddy? Who would you pair them up with?

Would Benefit: "Buddy" with:

_____   _____

_____   _____

_____   _____

_____   _____

_____   _____

_____   _____

_____   _____

NOTES:

Go for No!® Leader Performance Driver #4
Challenge Your People Outside Their "Comfort Zones"

▼

Welcome to the longest section in this workbook. In a few minutes you'll understand why it is.

We've all heard the term "comfort zone," but what exactly does it mean? More importantly, how can you—as a team leader—challenge your people to get out of theirs?

The comfort zone is exactly what it sounds like—the places, actions, and routines that people are comfortable with: taking the same route to work every day, going to the same restaurants, ordering the same things off the menu every time, etc.

The thing to understand is that comfort zone patterns and routines don't happen by accident—they are the brain's way of helping us minimize stress, reduce risk, and create a state of mental and physical security. Unfortunately, the consequence of reducing stress and risk is that we also reduce opportunities for growth, development and reward. And this is a problem.

Understanding the problem, however, is worthless without finding a viable solution. Fortunately, that solution was discovered over 100 years ago in the research conducted by psychologists Robert M. Yerkes and John D. Dodson.

Yerkes and Dodson wanted to know: *How does one escape a state of comfortable stagnation and return to a state of uncomfortable growth?*

And the solution they discovered is ridiculously so simple it is easily ignored.

For people to experience growth, the kind of growth that leads to a steady level of increased performance, they need to be forced into what Yerkes and Dodson described as a state of *optimal anxiety.*

The answer is in understanding how muscle is built.

How Muscle Is Developed

Ask anyone how muscle is built and the majority of people will say *weightlifting.* And they'd be wrong. Muscle is <u>not</u> developed by lifting weights—*it's built during the recovery period that follows.*

Weightlifting creates small, microscopic tears in the muscle, which is why your muscles ache for a few days afterwards. But what happens next is literally a miracle. After a weightlifting session the body goes about the process of repairing the damaged muscle and—in the process—makes it stronger.

Yerkes and Dodson's big discovery was the realization that people's comfort zones don't expand while they are experiencing anxiety outside of it, but afterward, during recovery. It is during the period of safety that the brain is rewired to think, *"That wasn't too bad. Nothing disastrous happened. Let's try that again!"*

Go for No! Rewires the Brain

On a surface level, Go for No! is a numbers game, right? Increasing the number of NOs someone hears leads to more yeses. This part is easy to understand; it's just numbers. But where the process gets really interesting is in how *rewiring of the brain* takes place.

When a person with a limited comfort zone is challenged to increase the number of times they hear YES, pressure and anxiety is increased. As a result, they race back to the comfort zone. But when we make the initial goal to simply hear NO more often, NO becomes a goal rather than an obstacle. When they hear a NO, the brain says, *"Okay, this is good. Keep going."* This helps people stay outside the comfort zone for longer and longer periods of time.

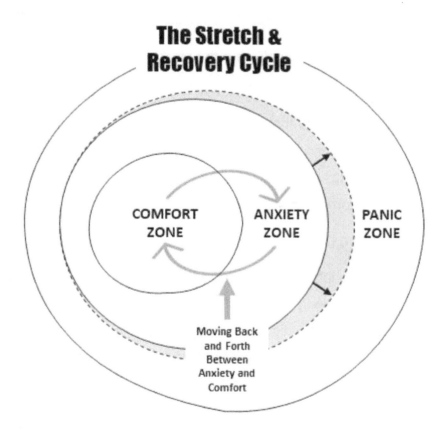

Short Bursts of "Doable" Challenges

When people are exposed to too much anxiety, and for too long a period, they become too stressed to perform. Rather than improving performance, productivity drops off. Sometimes sharply. This is obviously not what you're trying to achieve.

No one can live outside their comfort zone all the time. People need time to retreat to a place where they process their experiences while they were outside the comfort zone.

The answer is to challenge people outside their comfort zones for short periods—short bursts of optimal anxiety—followed by a return to the safety of the comfort zone.

Three Specific Ways to Challenge the "Comfort Zone"

Here are three specific ways you can challenge people outside their comfort zones. (Note: all three of these are covered in detail in our 21-Day Challenge Workbook which can be used by each member of your team to stretch their individual comfort zones. For more details visit our store at www.goforno.com).

1... Setting NO-Goals™

Everyone knows what YES-Goals are—they're goals set specifically to close more sales, increase revenue, and/or achieve some other desired outcome, all of which is the result of getting someone to say "YES." What we're talking about here is setting *NO-Goals*—goals for the number of times people say NO and *reject* the offer.

One of the side benefits of setting NO-Goals is how it keeps people in the game when things are going well (no, that is not a typo). For example: Someone sets a goal to make 10 sales during a given month, and they achieve that goal in just two weeks. They're not just on a winning streak, they're on fire! Everyone they approach says YES to them! So what do they do? They slow down. Maybe they even stop. And why not? They hit their YES goal for the month already.

Now, imagine the same person set a goal to get 100 NOs for the month, and they've only gotten 35 NOs so far. If this were the case, they wouldn't be ahead—they'd be behind! Rather than slowing down, they'd have to *increase* their prospecting and sales activity in order to reach their NO-Goal.

Now, you may be wondering: *"What should a person's NO-Goal be?"* This is impossible for us to answer, because one size does not fit all. Every business/sales situation is different. And it's the same with people. One person's comfort zone will vary greatly from the next. So we *can't* tell you what the goal should be, because we don't know your business nor do we know your people.

But you do.

You know your business, and you know your people.

Help them to set goals that are realistic yet will cause the person to stretch. And don't set them based on what YOU could do—base the goal around what *they* can do. What you find to be easy may paralyze someone else. It takes a lot of courage for some people to break out of their comfort zone, so start slow. Don't demand too much too quickly. Asking someone to get 100 NOs, when doing so is unrealistic for even your best performers, will have the opposite effect you're looking for.

Remember, you are challenging *their* comfort zone, *not yours.* The action you are asking someone to take doesn't have to be risky and stressful to *you*, only to *them*. You must see the world though *their* eyes and adjust accordingly. Don't challenge the team, challenge each individual.

2... The "One More Call" Challenge

Another great way to get people to implement Go for No! as a best practice is to encourage every member of your team to adopt a "One More Call" mindset. And it's really simple. Just instruct them to…

> **"At the end of the day, when you're ready to go home, make just one more call."**

But there's a twist. Don't just challenge your people to make one extra call per day, but to make those calls to prospects they think are likely to say NO to them. Not only will this generate additional sales, it will establish a direct connection between *'going for no'* and tangible results.

As sales guru Jeb Blount of SalesGravy.com says: *"The impact of those extra calls was mind blowing. So many of my 'one more calls' turned into sales. It was as if the universe was rewarding me for sticking to it."*

The numbers don't lie. When people make "one more call" a day, 5 days a week (meaning 200+ extra calls per year!) at even a modest closure rate of 20%...

Well, you can do the math.

Be sure to instruct the people on your team to keep track of the number of extra calls they make, as well as the results they got for their effort. Then have people share their experience with other members of the team in sales meetings, on team calls, etc. When those who are slow to get onboard see the results others are getting, they'll realize Go for No! isn't simply a catchphrase—it produces results.

3... The Go for No!® 21 Day Challenge

One of the ways to get people out of their comfort zones and make it fun is by conducting a Go for No! 21 Day Challenge.

The best part is the challenge is easy to coordinate and run because it's exactly what it sounds like: having people collect as many NOs as they can over a three-week period, keeping track of the numbers, and then reporting/sharing the results.

Again, to aid in this process, we created The 21-Day Go for No! Challenge workbook which can be used by each member of your team in which they set NO-Goals and track their results.

(For more details visit our store at www.goforno.com).

If for some reason you elect not to use the workbooks, here are the four main elements of the challenge:

- **Step One:** Have people count the number of NOs they hear over a three- week period to establish a "baseline" number of NOs they'll want to exceed during the challenge period.

- **Step Two:** Using the number of NOs they've established in Step One, have people set a NO-Goal—a number of NOs to shoot for—during the challenge.

- **Step Three:** Have people start the challenge, keeping meticulous track of the number of NOs they hear, as well as the results they generate.

- **Step Four:** Have team members analyze the results, tally the totals, and share them with you and (if you desire), others.

Make sure the 21 days of the challenge is free of major events and/or distractions, such as holidays or business conferences, etc., in order to get an apples-for-apples comparison of the results and to avoid having things that will slow momentum.

The 20/60/20 Rule

So how many of the people on your team will embrace the Go for No! message and truly implement it? First, accept that your chances of getting 100% of your people to be 100% on board with any training initiative are literally zero (unless you have a very small, micro-managed team.) This is where the 20/60/20 Rule comes in, which says:

- **20%** of people who are exposed to any new idea/concept will accept it and utilize it, either in full or in part.

- **60%** of people will say they like what they hear and agree with it, but they will need to be challenged to overcome their fears and self-imposed limitations to put the concept into action.

- **20%** of people will not embrace the concept or change their behavior, no matter what you say, do or try.

But you know this already, right? Because you've experienced it over and over in the past. The percentages may be off slightly, but probably not by much. These numbers hold true for just about any team or organization.

... determined by what you do with ... ews is, once you get people to ... brief periods on a regular basis, ... riencing these periods of optimal ... hese challenges so much, they'll ... ge themselves, all on their own.

Challenge Your Top Performers, Too

There's no doubt that some members of your team have superior selling skills, allowing them to close more sales more quickly than others. The question is, *what are they doing with the time savings?* Are they using the extra time to make even more calls to produce even more success, or do they slow down their prospecting and sales activity once their goals have been met?

Some of your best people may be using their superior skills to minimize the time spent selling, when they should be maximizing it. In effect, they are engaging in NO-avoidance just like everyone else, coasting along undetected, because they are hitting the goals and/or quotas you've set for them.

And the Bottom 20%?

Finally, how do you deal with the 20% of the people who simply won't get on board at all—the people who display negativity, especially in public, and with other members of your team? We're not going to tell you what to do, That's not our role. But it's probably time for a conversation about performance.

Expect People to Push Back

Any time a new program is introduced, you can expect that some people on your team will object to it, no matter how effective or logical the information or training may be. It's not that it might happen—*it will happen.* So it's a good idea to be prepared for it.

Below is a list of the common things people will push back on when it comes to Go for No! and possible ways to respond.

■

Common Objection: "If I'm pushy and aggressive, people will hate me."

Recommended Response: "No one is suggesting you become a pushy/aggressive salesperson that forces things on prospects. That is not what Go for No! is about. It's about making sure we recommend anything and everything that *is* in the customer's best interest. You can be *assertive* without being manipulative and *aggressive.* It's about *collecting decisions* from prospects, not manipulating them."

■

Common Objection: "I thought the purpose of selling was to get a yes."

Recommended Response: "Of course you're trying to get to a YES and should not be secretly hoping or praying for a NO. But getting to that YES requires you to be willing to go through the NOs to get there. Yes and No are not opposites, they are opposite sides of the same coin. (Note: The subtitle of the book *Go for No!* is: *Yes is the Destination, No is How You Get There.*)"

■

Common Objection: "Isn't Go for No! negative thinking?"

Recommended Response: "No, it's taking the negative reality that not everyone will tell you yes and making the act of hearing 'NO' positive and empowering. The fact is, the NOs are out there—the question is, how do you want to handle them?"

(Interesting note: Norman Vincent Peale said, "A positive thinker does not refuse to recognize the negative; he refuses to dwell on it. Positive thinking is a form of thought which habitually looks for the best results from the worst conditions.")

■

Common Objection: "I don't have time to increase the number of NOs I'm hearing."

Recommended Response: "Saying you don't have time to hear NO is like saying, 'You don't have time to sell.'"

Secondary response: "Wow, this must mean your in-box and voice mail are overflowing with messages from people who are desperate to buy. If that were the case, you'd be 300% over your goal. Chances are good that what you're too busy with are tasks and admin work that is keeping you from selling."

◼

Common Objection: "This idea of tracking the number of NOs I'm hearing is stupid and takes too much time."

Recommended Response: "Tracking NOs is only as complicated or as time consuming as you make it. You don't need any fancy system. You can make hash marks on a piece of paper if you want. And knowing that number lets us both get a much better look at your performance."

◼

Common Objection: "Following up with people who have told me NO in the past will make me look pushy and desperate."

Recommended Response: "Following up is part of the job, period. In today's world, persistence is a requirement for success. People who choose not to follow up with prospects will lose out to those that do."

◼

Common Objection: "I can't get any NOs because of voice mail! I leave messages, but no one ever gets back to me."

Recommended Response: "This is something everyone deals with, which makes finding ways to get to prospects more important than ever. If something is not working, try something else. Get creative. Mix up your approach. Try, test, fail, and try again. If voice mail is an issue, you need to work at crafting better, prospect-centric messages that compel people to call you back."

■

Common Objection: "Go for No! treats selling like a numbers game rather than treating people like people."

Recommended Response: "While people should never be looked at as "numbers" in a numbers game, understanding the numbers aspect of selling is important. Choosing relationships over selling is a false choice. You can be someone who builds relationships <u>and</u> focuses on getting results. This is what the ADVISOR selling style is all about."

■

Common Objection: "Approaching 100 prospects and getting 100 NO's is stupid—a total waste of time."

Recommended Response: "You're right, that would be stupid, and no one is suggesting you should. You're not trying to get NOs for the sake of simply hearing NO more often, you're doing it to increase the chances of hearing YES. And to that point: If you *do* speak to 100 people and get 100 NO's, the real question needs to be, why? Why did that happen? Chances are good it means you need to work on the QUALITY of your sales presentation in addition to the QUANTITY of calls you're making. Additionally, the prospects you're approaching simply aren't qualified, which is another problem altogether."

■

Common Objection: "Great salespeople never hear NO."

Recommended Response: "That's simply ridiculous. If you believe great salespeople never hear NO, you're living in a fantasy world. And anyone who really isn't hearing NO is going after easy sales, the low hanging fruit, and not challenging themselves by going for big NOs."

Analysis & Action Steps
for Performance Driver #4...

- Make a list of the people on your team, placing them each in one of the 20/60/20 categories:

BOTTOM 20%...   **MIDDLE 60%...**   **TOP 20%...**

_____   _____   _____

_____   _____   _____

_____   _____   _____

_____   _____   _____

(*Use additional paper or Excel spreadsheet to make a more complete list.)

- What is your plan for challenging the Middle 60%?

_____

_____

_____

- What do you intend to do about the bottom 20%?

_____

_____

_____

Go for No!® Leader Performance Driver #5

Celebrate "Success Behaviors" Even When They Fail to Deliver Results

I t's common for people to celebrate when they win, when they achieve success. What's not so common is to celebrate the attempt itself, especially when that attempt was not successful. The result is the feeling that YES is good, which it is, and that NO is bad, which it isn't—not if you believe that YES is the destination, but NO is how you get there.

Most team leaders avoid celebrating failure (specifically hearing NO from a prospect/customer) because of the belief that doing so will result in an *increase* in the number of NOs being heard. The truth is, *yes*, it will. And that's the point.

Encouraging someone to keep going when they're hearing nothing but "NO" is important in three ways:

1. It helps to keep people in the game long enough to master the skills they need to eventually achieve success.

2. When success *does* finally arrive, it validates the connection between YES and NO.

3. It balances the emotional reaction people experience when hearing YES and NO.

All three are critical factors to helping people with a fear of failure and rejection.

The <u>NEW</u> Model for Getting Behavior Change

For the better part of the last 200 years, the accepted model for getting behavior change from others was a four-step process that looked something like this:

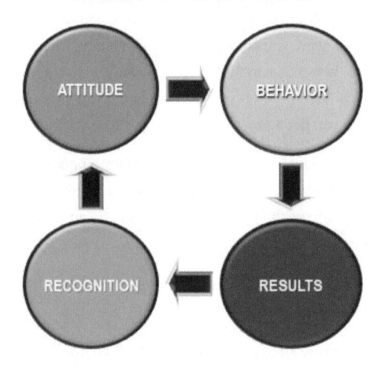

The <u>Traditional</u> Approach for Getting Behavior Change & Results...

The idea is, if you talked to people and explained what they should be doing differently, they'd be motivated to change their behavior. Then the new behavior would lead to results. At this point leaders jump in and provide recognition for the results achieved in the form of awards, prizes, money, etc. Sound familiar?

Here's the thing, though: research has determined this is <u>not</u> the most efficient way to get behavior change from others. There's a shortcut.

The best way to get behavior change from others is this:

The <u>More</u> <u>Effective</u> Model...

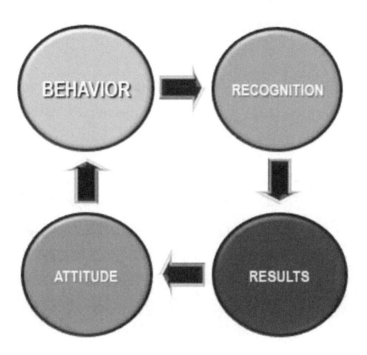

This approach suggests that the very first thing a team leader should do to get behavior change is to focus on getting people to change their behavior, but not by talking at them. Trying to get people to change their behavior through logic and reasoning is the long way—a way that rarely leads to the results you're looking for.

What we're suggesting, as far as Go for No! is considered, is this:

Step One: Challenge your people outside their comfort zones by insisting they gather more NOs from their prospects and customers and hold them accountable to doing it.

Step Two: The minute they start increasing the number of NOs they hear, immediately recognize them for the effort... *regardless of the results.* Do not wait for the behavior to produce results to recognize it. Recognize it anyway.

Step Three: Continue recognizing the desired behavior whenever you see it or hear about it. This recognition will keep people engaging in the behavior until, finally, results are achieved (and here's where things get really interesting)...

Step Four: People's attitudes will change *on the back end* once they see results—not because you *told* them the results were possible, but because they see them for themselves.

> **GOOD** leaders reward people when they succeed.
>
> **GREAT** leaders also recognize people when they demonstrate success behaviors, **even when those behaviors fail to produce the desired result.**

A Great Sports Example

In their landmark book, *Whoever Makes The Most Mistakes Wins*, authors Richard Farson and Ralph Keyes go out of their way to make the point that success and failure should be treated alike. They point out that even the terms success and failure are used sparingly by enlightened managers and rewarding one and punishing the other creates more problems than it solves. Which can be a difficult idea to embrace.

As an example, they mention how, *"During Olympic volleyball games, win or lose, teammates commonly shake hands with one another. Whether the players make the shot or miss, they are given the support and appreciation of the others. They treat failure and success the same way. We take that as a metaphor for good management."*

If you want people to embrace hearing NO more often, then celebrate the shot—regardless of the outcome.

Provide Motivation When Most Needed

When you think about it, the idea of celebrating the "success behavior" of *going for no,* even when it fails to deliver a positive result, makes perfect sense. After all, when do people need motivation the most:

When things are going well, or when things are going poorly?

To be clear, you, as a team leader, are <u>not</u> celebrating *failure*—you are celebrating *action.* And there's nothing that says you need to present an award to the person with the most NOs at your next sales conference, but if you did, you might be surprised to discover both the award for the most NOs and the most YESSES going to the same person.

Analysis & Action Steps
for Performance Driver #5...

- Make a list of various opportunities for celebrating the number of NOs your people hear (for example, on weekly team calls, newsletters, in emails, etc.)

_____

_____

_____

_____

_____

- Is it possible to create an award for the Top "NO-Getter?" If so, what would it be (a plaque? a trophy?)

_____

_____

_____

Go for No!® Leader Performance Driver #6

Commit to the Process & "Walk-the-Talk"

This final performance driver is short and easy to understand, but it may not be easy to do. Because it has nothing to do with your team—*it has to do with you.* And the best way to set it up is with an amazing story about Charles Blondin.

Blondin was a French tightrope walker who gained celebrity and fame in September 1860, as the first person to walk a tightrope stretched 11,000 feet (more than a quarter mile) over the roaring waters of Niagara Falls. Throngs of people from both United States and Canada traveled thousands of miles to see if he could do it. He did.

Not only did Blondin complete the feat, he did so multiple times, each time making it more difficult than the last. He did it in the dark, blindfolded, on stilts, in a burlap sack—one time he even did it on a bicycle. And every time he completed the challenge, people wanted even more, which led one time to him doing it pushing a stove upon which he cooked an omelet as he traversed the rope!

One day, Blondin crossed the tightrope pushing a wheelbarrow filled with a sack of potatoes during a rainstorm in a howling wind. It was extremely dangerous, but he did it because he never wanted to disappoint a crowd. And it was at the end of this performance that someone challenged him to cross the falls pushing the wheelbarrow a second time. Blondin declined. But the man persisted in his challenge. "What's wrong, Blondin," the man taunted, "do it!"

Blondin stopped and addressed the man, asking: "Do you really believe I can do it?"

"Yes," the man shouted.

"Okay," Blondin replied, "then get in the wheelbarrow."

Are You Willing To Get In The Wheelbarrow?

The story about Charles Blondin and the wheelbarrow illustrates an important point. If you want anyone to do anything—especially if the thing you want them to do is new and a bit scary—you need to be a leader who doesn't simply *talk-the-talk*, you need to *walk-the-walk*.

Telling people to do something you, yourself, are not willing to do is pointless. It will never work.

People respect leaders when they lead by example. Want people to work long hours? Then you have to work long hours. Want people to master the art of closing deals? Then you have to master the art, too. And if you want people to be willing to hear NO more often, then you need to go for no yourself.

Get in the trenches.

Show them how it's done.

Set the example.

Analysis & Action Steps
for Performance Driver #6...

List three ways in which you can increase and demonstrate your commitment to Go for No! to your team.

1) _____

_____

_____

2) _____

_____

_____

3) _____

_____

_____

Finally, we'll leave you with the words of French poet Guillaume Apollinaire:

> *"Come to the edge,"* he said.
>
> They said, *"We are afraid."*
>
> *"Come to the edge,"* he said.
>
> They came.
>
> He pushed them...
>
> And they flew.

Maybe it's time to push your people to fail more—to take a few more risks, but always in the prospect's best interest.

If you do, what they achieve might surprise you.

And themselves.

They may even fly.

ABOUT RICHARD & ANDREA...

Richard Fenton and Andrea Waltz are the founders of Courage Crafters, Inc. and authors of the best-selling book, *Go for No!*®

Speaking on stage together in a unique two-person style of delivery, Richard and Andrea teach people how to reprogram the way they think about the word no to get better results faster while building their courage and confidence. They share specific ways to apply their Go for No! strategy on a daily basis, creating a mindset that encourages tenacity and persistence, especially during tough times.

Before launching their company over 20 years ago, Richard learned to sell at the country's largest fleet dealer from a true master—his father. Andrea originally wanted to work with George Lucas but after getting rejected (she was 8) she went on to build a career in sales and management, meeting Richard at LensCrafters where they decided to launch Courage Crafters. Today, Go for No! has become well-known in the world of sales performance training and is widely recognized as the singular best program of its kind.

Their concepts have been featured in hundreds of online and offline publications, including FORBES and SUCCESS MAGAZINE. After hitting #1 on Amazon's Sales & Selling Best Seller list in 2010, their book has remained in the top 50 sales books for the last ten years, earning over 1,000 5-star reviews.

Organizations who've benefited from having Richard and Andrea speak to their people include American Express, Mobile Mini, The Pampered Chef (US, Canada & UK), OneHope Wine, Jiffy Lube, Lemongrass Spa, Public Storage, Tervis, American Tire Distributors, Utility Warehouse Ltd., Harry & David, Ameriplan, Lifetouch, and many more.

For more information on the Go for No!® program, visit www.GoforNo.com

For information on having Richard and Andrea speak to your group, visit: www.GoforNoKeynote.com

THE BOOK THAT STARTED IT ALL!

Sticks and Stones May Break My Bones but "NO" Can Never Hurt Me! That's the lesson twenty-eight-year old copier salesman Eric James Bratton is about to learn. And he's going to learn it from the most unlikely of mentors—himself!

Imagine going to bed one night, then to awaken the next morning in a strange house with no idea of how you got there. Only this house doesn't belong to just anyone—it belongs to you: a wildly successful future version of the person you might one day become, providing you are willing to start doing one simple thing. And that thing is?

To be willing to hear the word NO more often.

Before the weekend is over Eric will learn…

- What it takes to outperform 92% of the world's salespeople

- That failing and being a "failure" are two very different things

- Why it's important to celebrate success and failure

- The five failure levels and how to progress through them

- How to get past failures quickly and then move on

- That the most empowering word in the world is not yes—it's NO!

- And much, much more!

These lessons are destined to change the way he thinks, the way he sells, and the way he lives forever. And they'll do the same for you!

Available on AMAZON.com. For information on quantity discounts, call 1-800-290-5028 or email us at: Infor@GoForNo.com

THE GO FOR NO!® 21 DAY CHALLENGE

What level of performance could your team achieve in just 21 days if the only thing they did was to intentionally increase the number of times they heard the word NO?

That's the core concept behind the *Go for No! 21 Day Challenge!*

The Challenge:

1. Ensures participants put the Go for No! strategies into immediate action.

2. Provides a mechanism for monitoring and tracking results.

3. Motivates people by providing immediate, tangible results!

This 80-page workbook is perfect as a follow-up tool to our keynote presentation or used as an action-oriented companion to the book.

Available on AMAZON.com. For information on quantity discounts, call us at 1-800-290-5028 or email us at: Info@GoForNo.com.

Made in the USA
Columbia, SC
23 May 2022